Death Mother and Other Poems

Books by Frederick Morgan

Death Mother and Other Poems (1979)

The Tarot of Cornelius Agrippa (1978)

Poems of the Two Worlds (1977)

A Book of Change (1972)

Death
Mother
and Other Poems

Frederick Morgan

University of Illinois Press *Urbana, Chicago, London*

Grateful acknowledgment is made to the following publications in which poems in this book were first published: *America:* "Abenaki Poem," "Three Children Looking over the Edge of the World," "The Message"; *American Scholar:* "The Turtle," "February 11, 1977," "Eternity, I"; *Antioch Review:* "The End of the Story"; *The Atlantic:* "As It Was"; *Commonweal:* "Suspiria"; *Harper's:* "Death Mother," "After Shen Chou," "After Wen Cheng-ming," "After Su Shih"; *Hollow Spring Review:* "Eternity, II"; *The Hudson Review:* "Century Poem"; *The Listener:* "Samson"; *The Nation:* "At Midnight," "Breath," "The Ghost," "The Summit"; *New England Review:* "In Mexico," "Orpheus to Eurydice," "The Path"; *New York Arts Journal:* "'We took a room at the Westbury...,'" "A Bad One," "The Tiger"; *The New Yorker:* "The Turn," "President Poem"; *New York Review of Books:* "'Lucky black man in my dream...'"; *New York Times:* "The Busses"; *Ontario Review:* "The Snake"; *Poetry:* "Canandaigua"; *Sewanee Review:* "The Wedding in Cana of Galilee"; *Southern Review:* "History," "'Writing is simplicity...,'" "Thought," "The End"; *Tar River Poetry:* "The Trader"; *Virginia Quarterly Review:* "The Promise."

Library of Congress Cataloging in Publication Data

Morgan, Frederick, 1922–
   Death mother and other poems.

   I. Title.
PS3563.083D4   811'.5'4   79–17983
ISBN 0-252-00754-9
ISBN 0-252-00755-7 pbk.

For Paula

"... ave mundi rosa,
Blanziflor et Helena,
Venus generosa."

Contents

"Death's dreadful advent is the mark of man,
And ev'ry thought that misses it is blind."

One

Death Mother

for Hayden Carruth

1
You came as sleep, warily:
when I woke
things had a deep-blue look.

You disguised yourself as night, but
behind the stars
I saw dark flashes of your body.

And as for dreams—
how many you tried me with!
It seems you never weary of your
hopeful grim deceptions

as though I stood in need of such
visions of filth and blood
to move me to acknowledge your
dominion, mother.

2
Lady, when you were born—
frail, blue-veined from the womb
but destined by a god—
the proud man dashed you down.
You died before you lived

yet from the detested corpse
a raging spirit strode up into heaven,
and the man fell shuddering
seeing his death at large.

Now in the night sky
with breasts like elephants,
all circleted in moonbeams,
dark-skinned, in your delicate dark skirt
you dance out our black age.

3

Death is the least of things to be feared
because while we are it is not
and when it comes we are not
and so we never meet it at all.

That was a Greek way of avoiding the issue—
which is, that ever since the blood-drenched moment
of primal recognition,
death has lived all times in us
and we in her, commingled,
and not to recognize her is
not to recognize ourselves.

The lovely body is composed of what was dead
and will be dead again. Death
gives us birth, we live in her.

4

I cornered the thief in the garage at dusk.
Small, furry, with quick-darting eyes
he made no sound but watched his chance.

He had none. I took hold of a heavy stick
and when he rushed me, struck him once
and crushed his skull. There on the cement floor

all at once that life came to an end.
Out of the nostrils blood was oozing,
the right eye dripped down from its socket.

I felt revulsion at myself and him.
The dog edged up and nosed the body.
Later, in the dark, I dug a quiet grave,
laid him in it and covered him over,
and all was almost as if he had never been.

5

The breasts of the loving mothers flow with milk:
quiet in the streamside grove
they suckle the sacred children.
Sit, rest yourself for a moment in the cool of those trees
for it seems (on such a day) love must prevail.

But the Mother is playful and sportive,
she of the burial grounds:
at nightfall Helen the fair
in paroxysm of change
shrivels, a hag with withered dugs.

Do not think to escape her
by calling her fortunate name!
From her mouth blood pours in a torrent,
her girdle is human hands,
she frees one in a hundred-thousand—
the rest she holds to the game.

6

There was no bulldozer handy, so
we shoveled the corpses into the pit —
twenty of us on detail.

I can't remember which month it was, April or May.
The sun was out, a small breeze was blowing as usual.
It meant wading into a complex mass of rot,
they were so many and so putrefied,
with here and there a leg, an arm, a head.
We wore masks, but gagged even so —
several passed out.

Afterwards, where we filled the earth in, it bubbled,
and on the march back Kröger said, "My God,
I'd rather die than do that again."
But he didn't die. None of us did, just then.

7

You cast me from your filthy womb
where snails, worms, and leeches grow
and when I've finished out my time
back down your great gorge I'll go
into your black and stinking gut
and crouch there centuries and rot
and be excreted, or reborn—
it's all the same, it's you I'm from,
your stench, your blood, your pain and lust,
your beauty raising up my pride,
your eyes that gleam in murderous jest,
your ancient sluice that I've enjoyed.
How, mother mine, shall I grow free
of you who keep remaking me?

8

Is it useful to have a mythology of death
or handier just to get along with the bare idea,
the barer the better? Such as
a plain black nothingness: easy to think of
like a light going out. Why
get into talk of legends and deities
with all their paraphernalia?

I deny that consolation is the answer.
The greatest consolation (as Epicurus knew)
is the light going out. All notions
of continuance build up in us expectancy—
and *that* is perhaps the answer: life
as lived, responsive to its fiercest surge,
assumes its own indefinite extension...
He has not fully lived, Lorenzo de' Medici said,
who has not felt that other life to come—
and yet one must not dwell on it too much
or put on airs. The light goes out for sure

and all the rest is images—in whose mind?

9

One sweltering Sunday afternoon in August,
walking through the back-meadows as was my custom
I grew sleepy, and lay down in a patch of shade
to rest. Drowsed off; and had this dream I can't forget.

I saw a gigantic woman striding toward me
across the fields: glad eyes in a grim face
and crests of huge dark wings that loomed behind her.
She held in one hand a dripping sword, in the other —
dangling from the intermingled hair —
a thousand human heads confused and bunched.
I was the only person left alive,
and as she neared and looked into my eyes
I saw in hers my own self, burning bright.

This frightened me — my heart shook — and I woke.

10

Who will laugh
in coldest glee
when earth darkens once for all?

When graveyard meats
are the only food,
who will eat the dead men's faces?

And who rides free
in the night sky
holding the mirror that holds the world?

Is it not I
deep in the heart,
I who died before I lived?

Black one,
naked dancer on corpses,
with you as Mother
how shall we fear death.

Two

As It Was

Remember the old peasant of
Broadway and 19th—
scraped red face, a croaking smile and
twisted hands a size or two too large?

Huge-bottomed, she was bulked in swathes of black.
Heaved it all down on a grocer's crate most often—
not far from the corner, in front of the old bank.

I saw her winter evenings on my walks
in sharpest cold, sometimes in snow,
selling puppies from a big brown basket—
litters gummy-eyed and squeaking—
and candy too: gumdrops, licorice
a penny each, and oddly shaped dark cookies
ginger-tasting, dusted white with sugar.

It seemed to me she was old beyond the telling
but she never changed. I was the one who aged.
One day she simply wasn't there any more.

Years later, I thought of her when spring came round
and days grew long again:
how at Easter time she used to sell white rabbits,
and water lilies in mid-June.

The Turtle

In August 1932 it must have been.
The Bering Hill Road, outside of Greenwich, was dirt in those days
with here and there a big boulder poking through.
We eased along it carefully in the Marmon
those late afternoons, near dusk, when we went out searching.

I was ten years old. My mother—young, high-spirited—
loved birds and liked to drive, particularly that svelte old car of hers.
"Come on," she'd say, "let's see if we can find the scarlet tanagers!"—
for we liked the colorful kinds best, though towhees,
dickcissels, cedar waxwings, were all admired in their seasons—

and I'd climb in the front and slam the door, and off we went
out the back lanes and along the dusty Bering Hill Road
and sometimes we saw scarlet tanagers and more often we didn't
but almost always something strange and fine:
badgers, orioles, foxes, rose-breasted grosbeaks—once, an eagle.

—This particular afternoon was a hot one, that shimmered,
and we took our drive a bit earlier than usual.
It was a Sunday, I think—I remember the heat-haze
above pale green treetops, and the eddying road-dust.
After going along luckless for a while, we stopped the car

and got out and stretched—and it was then, down the road a ways,
that I saw something dark right out in the middle,
a mottled thing, rounded like a rock, but it had moved.
I ran over, knelt down, and to my joy it was alive!
—a big patient box-turtle, withdrawn into his fortress.

It's hard to describe the love I felt for him,
love, and fear too, in the freshness of wonder
as I touched the smooth hardness of brown patterned carapace
sensing beneath it a life somehow my own.
And then my mother called me to her: a car was coming.

It was an old Model-T with two young men in front.
It came rattling and clattering in a huge cloud of dust
and swerved in its course so as to run over the turtle:
as I watched, the wheel crunched him, he exploded, and the pieces
flew high in the air as they drove away laughing.

"They did it deliberately!" my mother cried out.
No more to be said, we drove home in silence—
but I've sheltered, since then, a certain hard knowledge
that has kept me from yielding spirit or mind
to hopeful assumptions of man's native goodness.

Canandaigua

Lake of green—
   those mornings in Canandaigua
I'd wake up on the sleeping-porch
with kittens walking all over me
tails up, purring . . . We
had five or six from one litter:
their bodies wove softly through our hands
and the children gave each one a name.
Came mid-August,
you crushed one under the car one day
starting up in a hurry,
and had five old-fashioneds for supper and cried all night.
At the end of summer we gave the rest back to a farmer.

Lake of green—
   Iroquois dawns—
I read Francis Parkman,
and Doktor Faustus in page proofs,
and after the morning swim
through water transparent and sleek in the buttery sun
sat on the point with a yellow pad
and tried my hand writing poems.
I started fifty or more, I guess,
but didn't finish one.

You wore your hair frizzy that summer.
You swam with your slow easy strokes
the lake you loved as a child,
then sunned yourself on the shore and removed your halter.
You were small and beautiful
and a hater of life always,
retaining in every word and act
a bitterness far too precious for you to surrender it.
And so you read Catholic books
and argued and were at loose ends
and drank down your bourbon old-fashioneds when the dusk came on.
You liked to undress in front of an open window

and one night, when the neighbors were having a cookout,
they all walked over to admire the view.

We had visitors—too many,
as people do who haven't made lives for themselves:
the blonde, your school friend, who struck attitudes
all day long in her tight white two-piece Jantzen—
the Village radical in tall cowboy boots
who stopped with his trailer on his way out West—
the "critic" (he later became the admen's adman)
who, rolling his eyes at the hills across our lake,
emitted some bilge about earth navels and Indian totems.

The animals were more interesting.
I found occasional water rats—
self-reliant, a little slimy—
fat groundhogs and lithe otters,
and early one misty morning, lost in the garden,
a half-blind gray-furred mole.
Sometimes, at noon, a fish-hawk circled above us
and far far back in the hills ram-skulls could be found on high meadows.

Lake of green—
   late afternoons towards dusk
I'd take the children in the station wagon and drive
halfway back up the hill to the local dump,
and there went our garbage!—sacks, boxes, cans
into a green leafy gulch
as the kids, shouting and laughing,
took turns with me tossing it down.
And we rode back home singing songs—
"John Henry" and "Willy the Weeper"
and "I've Been Workin' on the Railroad"—
and had a last swim before supper.

At night cool air drifted in from the lake—
time for stories. As you sat with your drink,

I read aloud from A. A. Milne
or Oz or *The Wind in the Willows,*
and we'd kiss our dear ones goodnight and tuck them in,
and the evening was ours, it seemed . . .

Not so. Each evening was finally itself.
And ourselves were not ours, perhaps, but part of time's
endless elaborations of nothingness.
The days passed, the summer too,
and then it was over, all over, and we returned
to the city and a larger home in time,
and moved ahead through changing years,
and none of us ever went back to Canandaigua
except you—who are buried now
in the graveyard looking down on the lake from the top of the hill.

"We took a room at the Westbury..."

We took a room at the Westbury
and watched the summer rain pour down
all that long July afternoon...
It steamed in the streets...At seven o'clock
we moved on down to the bar for drinks.

We sat side by side on the black banquette.
When I touched your arm, you shuddered away
hissing your hate...Still, I could hear
steady outside the cleansing drench.

I let my mind go wandering then
to your litanies of cheap despair,
poor bitch so urgent to be damned
(for it seemed you didn't want a friend
but only mirrors to behold your grief)

and all at once, on the second drink
(yourself still festering at my side)
caught sense of something waiting there—

something that seemed alive
this side the curtains made of rain
yet occupying no certain space:
something that wore my dreaming face...

Madness, a demon or a god?
These days one never can be sure
or tell, even, the difference.
Whatever it was, *I* made its sense...

What did we do when dinner was over—
go to some third-rate movie or other,
then patch up a truce and head for bed?

That's how it went, as I recall.
In the sparse room we stripped and fucked
and sprawled in the bed-light, hearing the rain—

then, as we lay there lightly touching,
you offered the falsehood of your kiss.

Yes, each accepting the other's lie
we could neither forgive nor be forgiven...
But I'm sorry now, poor hateful child,
you found no easier rest that night
with one who awaited what still was hidden.

February 11, 1977

to my son John

You died nine years ago today.
I see you still sometimes in dreams
in white track-shirt and shorts, running,
against a drop of tropic green.

It seems to be a meadow, lying
open to early morning sun:
no other person is in view,
a quiet forest waits beyond.

Why do you hurry? What's the need?
Poor eager boy, why can't you see
once and for all you've lost this race
though you run for all eternity?

Your youngest brother's passed you by
at last: he's older now than you—
and all our lives have ramified
in meanings which you never knew.

And yet, your eyes still burn with joy,
your body's splendor never fades—
sometimes I seek to follow you
across the greenness, into the shade

of that great forest in whose depths
houses await and lives are lived,
where you haste in gleeful search of me
bearing a message I must have—

but I, before I change, must bide
the "days of my appointed time,"
and so I age from self to self
while you await me, always young.

Suspiria

Take them, death—take
whoever belongs to you:
your likeness is stamped
inwardly, on the plasm.

The mass of flesh and bone
absorbs into the soil;
consciousness, too, is renewed,
pale in its billion cells.

The single life blossoms,
fades, drops to the earth,
as the tree lives on in the dream
by which it is remembered.

Three

Abenaki Poem

To make the deerskin shirt for her husband
first she dipped the skin
in a bucket of strong lye
prepared from wood-ash and hot water:
this made it easier to remove the hair.

She then stretched it out across a square
upright frame of branches tied at the corners
and fastened to poles stuck in the ground.
Squatting before this frame
she scraped the hair from the skin
with a tool fashioned of muskrat bone:
its upper end was secured to a wooden handle,
its lower edge carved into serried teeth.

The skin having been scraped clean, she rubbed it briskly
with brains of the selfsame deer
and smoked it in a thick smudge made from rotten wood:
the shirt could now be counted on
to retain its suppleness
even when drenched by rain or river water ...

Not much game in the forests of the northeast
that winter (the nights were dark and thick with owls):
a few deer killed, raccoons trapped,
from time to time fish hooked through holes in the ice—
and once a black bear treed and slaughtered.

Counting the children, they were eight in that family.
The men held to the old ways
but she had heard strange whisperings in the north—
and at night as the fire dimmed,
when she had prayed to her manito
and to the evil one abroad by day and by dark,
she added a phrase or two for the new weak god—
the anxious one who dangled from her neck.

The Colonist

As I write you, dear friend,
I turn my thoughts to home—not
in longing, be it said, or remorse
(for I feel nothing of these)
but in pleasant recollection of our childhood joys
and the hopes we shared as young men.

I was fifty years of age when I came to the Province
with wife and six children,
leaving only my eldest son at home to make his own way,
and here I have prospered, and here I expect to die,
and never return. Let my bones remain
in the soil of this dawning world...
I have no longing, no nostalgia,
for home to me was bitter ground,
my father's land and wealth used up
in litigations with the lairds
who would take my little to add to their much—
and the lairds' friends were the judges!
Dear Sir, how do you survive?
Our homeland is the prey of wolves and jackals.

But here, all is different—new.
I could not have imagined a climate so fine and healthy.
The air is sweet and clear, we find an agreeable smell,
and the sky seems much farther distant from us than at home.
Summers are ruled by the southwest wind—
the northwest governs the winters,
which continue from December to March and are most agreeable
with a fine pure sky and bright heavens
and seldom such black foul weather as we find at home...
No storms either, but fine small breezes—
and no great rains to rot the corn.

As for the soil, some parts of it are rich and some poor,
just as in other countries,

and if it is well improved and manured, it will bear good crops.
The majority of farmers here are lazy:
they make no improvement on their land
but just what they do with the plough, in which they are not very
    expert.
Many of them do not so much as draw
out to the land the dung which is made by their cattle.
When I arrived, I found, in several heaps by the house,
all the dung that had been made in the space of eleven years.
I was glad to find such copious ready manure
and drew it out to the land, where the results
were answerable to my pains and expectations,
for I had that year a rich crop:
wheat, rye, and Indian corn.

I need not tell you, Sir, for you know it already,
that we have no tithes or general taxes here,
or poor rates, or mill mulcters, or suchlike grievances
as tend to relax the diligence of the farmers.
We are privileged indeed: we choose of ourselves
our ministers, schoolmasters, constables, and all other parish officers
for laying and collecting all necessary assessments.
They are chosen by a majority of our votes.
In our neighborhood, if differences arise
about roads and marches, they are amicably adjusted
without process of law . . . But our courts themselves
are worthy of honest men.
Justice is impartially administered:
the poor are not browbeaten,
nor borne down by the rich.
And best of all, dear friend, our laws
are made by those who are not nominally only,
but in veriest fact our representatives:
for without bribes or pensions they are chosen
by ourselves—and every freeholder has a vote.

God must intend some good from all of this . . .
Dear Sir, how I wish that you yourself were present

to view with your own two eyes the things I speak of—
so, too, that I might have the solid pleasure
of clasping once again your hand!
How can I express the beauty
of the summer season here—
it is so fine, so healthful, and so pleasing?
While I and my sons are clearing ground,
and go for a while to walk, or rest ourselves
in the forest among the tall oaks on a summer day,
the sight of the heavens and the smell of the air
give me a pleasure which I cannot tell you
how great it is! When I sit down to rest,
the breezes of the southwest wind
and the whispering noise it makes in the top of the trees,
with the fine smell of the plants and flowers,
please me so exceedingly, that
I am as it were enchanted, and
unwilling to part from such a joy.

And so it is, old friend, that I do not wish to come home,
but will remain here to the end,
when—I pray—my soul will go to the enduring city,
and my body rejoin this soil which it has loved.

The Trader

"You'll be wanting a woman," Cavanaugh said with a laugh,
"a young strong fellow like you, and as soon as possible."
My first day here on the island it was—a hot one—
and he'd been on hand at the waterside when we landed
and seen about having my goods fetched up to the station.
I had from the first a feeling I'd like the place—
the village spread out like a crescent along the beach,
the thatched native houses crouched under sloped brown roofs,
and a crest of forest piling up thick behind.
The station was made of coral—the best house in town.

After he gave me lunch we sat for a while
drinking and getting acquainted on the verandah,
and he told me how glad he was to be going home.
"Twenty years is a damn long time, by God—
I've almost forgotten what Cincinnati looks like—
but you'll find I've left things here in pretty good order."
Then, after giving me tips as to local customs
and the strengths and weaknesses of the chief men in town,
he brought up this sudden business of a woman.

I didn't quite know what to say, so I only mumbled
"Sounds good to me," or something like that. "Why sure,"
he said, "you can have your pick. Come along right now."
And we took a walk through the village, in sunshine and shade,
and wherever we went the brown naked children straggled
behind us, crowing and chirping like so many chickens.
I took closer notice then of the island women:
they seemed right friendly, in their red and blue missionary dresses,
but they were brown—no getting around it—and they ran to fat.

We had almost finished the rounds when I saw to one side
a girl who looked better than the others. She was tall, slim,
with shy pale eyes like a vixen's, and had just come in
from fishing, or so I guessed, because her shirt stuck to her.
"She'll do," I said. "Very good," said Cavanaugh,
"I'll marry you tonight and be on my way tomorrow."
"Marry us?" I asked. "Do you mean you're some kind of parson?"

"Hell no," he answered, "but I keep an old Bible handy,
and I'll fix up a table real nice, covered with white cloth,
and light a few candles, and start reading anywhere at all
loud and dramatic, and it always goes over big.
It ain't legal, that's certain, but these folks don't know any better."

So that's how it was. I was "married" that same night
and left in sole charge next day when Cavanaugh sailed
and had Loana to sleep with and fix my meals.
I reckoned her a pretty good woman right from the start,
better than the run of that lot, because she did her best
to please me, and keep things neat, and had a knack for cooking,
and I didn't have to slap her around more than two or three times
when she started jawing at me while I was trying to think—
she soon caught on that I don't like noise when I'm thinking...

Well—I'd been here only two months, doing very good business
and getting along on the whole just fine with the natives,
when I came down with fever. Oh God, was that a misery!
Three days I burned and was out of my head and raved
and puked up my guts and sweated and stank and babbled
and changed to a boy again chased by filthy brown devils
and felt horrid hell dense and thick all around and inside me.
Then I'd come to myself for a moment and see her face
hanging over me like a dark moon, peaceful and quiet—
sometimes she'd be wiping my head with a moistened cloth,
sometimes it was food she'd be trying to get me to swallow—
I'd see her face through the mist, all dusky and calm,
and I'd have a great thought, which glowed, but then lose it entirely,
and sink back again into that stinking swamp.
The last night was the worst. I was trapped in tunnels of ice,
my teeth rattling my skull, and this fear inside me
that I had died, and was dying again in hell.
Oh, I shook so hard I thought I'd be snapping my neck!

It passed in the night. I woke up weak as a baby
with dawn in the room, my head clean-swept and cool,
and a vast soft weight on my body . . . Raising my hands, I fought free
of blankets, carpets, scarves, and reams of cloth
that were heaped up in huge drifts to keep me warm.
Then something rustled down on the floor beside me
and slowly raised itself to the morning light.
"Hello," I said. "Are you well?" she said. "Thank God.
I'll go get food now, you lie still right there."
She brought the soup in, helped me get some down
and took a few gulps herself. I could see she was hungry.
"Tell me the truth now," I asked. "How long since you've eaten?"
"Three days. I couldn't swallow while you were sick."
Her words didn't have any special kind of twist to them,
but they made me feel something sudden and strong inside.
"Old lady," I said, "you're almost as good as a Christian!"
—a fool thing to say, in a way, because she *was* a Christian—
I mean, she was a missionary convert like the others
and dressed herself up on Sundays and went to church
and listened to the native preacher and sang hymns,
which was more than I ever did—but I was born one
and she wasn't, and that makes a difference, you can believe me!
Anyway, my saying it pleased her very much.

I had a new feeling for Loana after that.
I always liked her, but now it was that, and different . . .

One day six weeks later I was back in the store checking stock
when I heard her voice sounding out real angry and strong
as if she was quarreling, which wasn't like her at all.
I ran around front—there she was, squared off with a native,
a fat oily brute who was calling her bad names in Kanaka.
"Just a minute," I said, "don't you cuss my old lady that way."
He cut short his yapping and gave me a black, ugly look,
then grabbed her wrist and started to pull her away!
Well, I soon stopped that. He was one of her uncles, it seems,

trying to shame her for setting up house with a white man.
My fist settled him. I may not have broken his jaw,
but it's certain he hasn't been bothering us again.

It's been seven full months, and we're used to each other's ways.
When she looks at me now, she smiles—much more than before—
like she's happy, I guess. But I, I can still see her face
quiet and brown, looking down at me in my swamp.
I found something then, if only I could have held on to it!

You work, you eat, you sleep—the days go by fast—
but when I'm alone in-between times, I've been thinking.
The missionary stops off here every two or three months
making his round of the islands, inspecting his flock.
I don't hold with them much, they're a poor weak sort of man mostly,
but I'm thinking next time of asking this one to stay over
and march himself up to the station here at mid-day.
We'll give good welcome and pay him a couple of smackers
and have him walk out with the two of us on the verandah—
with the village people standing in a crowd outside,
the men in green wreaths, the women all decked out in flowers,
and sun shining bright and wind blowing clean from the ocean—
and he'll marry me up to Loana right and proper.

History

I give you a Caribbean isle of seventy years ago,
a tropic night,
a ship anchored in the bay.
The sailors are drinking rum and thinking about women.

Strumming sounds drift across the water with the scent of hibiscus.
The moon is huge,
but do you not sense the soft
scene's desolation? Of sailors who sadly chat and drink,

of brown-skinned women paddling out in the small boats to trade with
    them,
and of lost homes
cast away in the cold lands
of snowy New England, or Illinois, or Nebraska?

The bodies will mingle, but how may we mingle their histories?
The night is mute,
while far back in his cabin
the captain, who has enjoyed a woman, thinks about hell.

In Mexico

Our mood had dissipated: a restless night,
   desires unfulfilled.
I slept on the chaise in the angle of the porch.
When morning came, clear and brilliant,
it brought its usual smells of cooking meat.

I shall do some heads of you in the Aztec sun,
   Serena,
or perhaps, forget it all
this one last glittering day
and bury my head in the fur between your thighs
and fuck, and sleep—
                    letting it all go by
until we go out at dusk to watch the cockfight.

Now a moist wind comes shuddering from the jungle:
what does it know of our moods, our complications?

The sun tells it all.
The sky is cruel.
Call it, if you like, a tragedy—
you leaning there against the whitewashed wall.
Have you not heard me whisper that I love you?

But, see, your lip is quivering:
a tear begins to fall.

The Wrong Side

The moon is partly hidden
by a white cloud drifting over—
and here, on the inside, by a white lace curtain.

You sit at a table with candles:
two red, one grey.
Your shaded face turns downward as you speak.

"Tell me," you ask softly,
"did he know that you were covering?
If so, I fear he must die.
Think carefully, please, before you reply."

The answer is plain enough
but I pause, and I listen to the wind
coldly shuffling through bare clumps of shrub.

"He must have known," I say,
"to have sent Jerome that message.
There is no other sense to it at all."

Your hand comes up from shadow—
you rest your head on it.
Your eyes close for a moment.
"We must arrange a way."

A servant brings in brandy
and hot spiced tea in glasses.
The curtains stir against the brilliant pane.

"The wrong side of the business,"
I say, glancing out at the moon.
I see you smile, reaching for the telephone.

Four

The Wedding in Cana of Galilee

The bride was beautiful
          Jesus thought—
but not for him, that
          softness of body,
fond slow richness of
          female elegance,
musk, perfume and
          tangling hair.

He felt already his
          desert of self
focused within to a
          point of light.
Was this the father's
          touch of fulfillment?
The view from the Skull
          would be his alone.

I may not enter you,
          woman of Galilee,
not in this life, not
          this side of the wind—
but see how my love for you
          stains the bright water
with blood of earth's vine
          of which I make free . . .

Woodwinds and drums: the
          maidens are dancing,
the guests glow with wine, the
          disciples give tongue.
The magician looks smiling
          on his dear folly,
reflecting on that
          into which he must change.

Samson

When Samson went in unto Delilah
God thundered ineffectually outside.
He could have stopped him in his tracks
but didn't choose to. Was it pride,

or was he just keeping up appearances,
hoping in his heart his champion would fall?
Perhaps he'd had enough of the tiresome exploits
of this bully-boy, forever spoiling for a brawl,

and judging that love, shame and hard times
would make the clown a more interesting friend,
prearranged the razor, the gouged-out eyes,
the enslavement in darkness—and if at the end

he restored for a moment that futile strength
it was only to bring home his lesson of despair—
for when all was suffered and told, the Lord
loved Samson more without his hair.

A Bad One

His eyes looked out from never a skull
but he plucked those reddish weeds
passionlessly in the half-glow
as dream ships foundered down the glade.

The moon wore the face of his long-lost love
beyond salt tides of a female night
whose creatures climbed his inward shores.

At the roots of the weeds worms wriggled
awaiting apocalyptic beaks.
He talked to himself, knowing no one was there
(having no tongue, his tongue was of air)
in mutterings shaped without teeth.

A long fat stalk was his sword in hand
to menace the fading sky:
he hugged his shadow-self goodbye

and fluttering up to the city of meat
where we last persons sleep snug in our heads
threads pale alleyways of bone
marking the lintels for death.

The Snake

Intoning syllables of wrath
        form then the image of a snake—
honor it with blue lotuses
        bathe it in the five ambrosias,
smear it with naga-quelling juice
        smear its head with golden ichor.

Lay it curled inside the pot
        filled with milk from a black cow,
wrap it in a woven cloth
        cut by the hand of a dark-skinned girl,
dig a trench to the northwest
        and place the hidden snake within.

Prepare your colors: BLACK will come
        from charcoal of the cemetery,
WHITE from the ground-up human bones.
        Cemetery bricks yield RED,
GREEN is from leaves of the caurya bush,
        DARK BLUE from bones and charcoal mixed.

Measure the mandala with the thread
        spun from intestines of a corpse,
lay it out truly point by point,
        image it in the prescribed colors—
at the center draw the God
        eight-faced, four-legged, trampling the serpent.

Dark trees mutter overhead
        while the snake's head swells with poison.
In that lonely place, alone,
        let the master, mind resolved
and centered on his inmost wrath,
        raise his hand to speak the mantra.

The Tiger

The tiger strides
            towards the city
which never
            (as far as you knew)
existed.

            It's walled in rock.
Somewhere inside
            an old man
slumbers
            coiled on his money.

Around it, fields
            of blue night-flowers
are tamped by
            fur of
soft paws padding

            as two eyes
watch
            from the stone sky:
one as moon
            the other moon's twin.

Secretly then
            by the hidden gate
two lovers
            flee
through rustling grasses

            (where once their
bodies
            merged as one)
into deep space
            of a tiger's gaze . . .

The city quivers
                in all its
granite
                readying for
a shift into time

                and the old king sucks
a black
                woman's breast
which turns to gold
                as the tiger leaps

The Promise

A million souls wandered out at midnight
into the Great American Nature Theatre,
a scooped-out place beneath Arizona stars.

Many held hands, all looked alike:
they had eaten their suppers of roadside meat,
the daily drug was bubbling in their ears.

In groups, intermingling, they drifted about
emitting their little shrieks of recognition
and exchanging such thoughts as they had had during the day.

"I had this nice thought," one of them would say,
"of how we are so much better off than the old ones—
because none of them knew what they were going to do

night after night after night until they died,
whereas we, my dears, are always assured,
each possessing the rest and all being of one mind."

"A lovely thought," the others would reply,
and kiss him solemnly—looking into his eyes—
and it became the Thought that was prized that night.

And then the stars went out as though a hand had snuffed them,
a million heads turned upward, and pictures came out in the sky:
billionaires in rocket-ships tempting the speed of light,

skiers on Everest, skin-divers off St. Croix,
firing-squads by the Amazon stained red with blood of the slain,
terrorists from Borneo blowing up Notre Dame—

and a voice came down from heaven that calmly explained
what each event meant, and why it was all the same
as what they had seen ten-thousand times before.

And at the very last, the President's face appeared
huge and pink, and as they all smiled and cheered,
he told them again that all was well,

that America was heaven and there was no hell—
though the rivers were poisoned, the lands burned dry,
the animals dead, and themselves about to die.

Three Children Looking over the Edge of the World

They came to the end of the road
and there was a wall across it
of cut stone—not very high.

Two of them boosted the third up
between them, he scrambled to the top
and found it wide enough to sit on easily.
Then he leaned back and gave the others a hand.

One two three in a row they sat there
staring: there was no bottom.
Below them a cliff went down and down for ever

and across from them, facing them, was nothing—
an emptiness that had no other side
and turned their vision back upon itself.

So there wasn't much to do or look at, after all.
One of them told a rhyme, the others chimed in,
and after a little while they swung around
and let themselves back down.

But when their feet touched solid road again
they saw at once they had dropped from the top of the sky
through sun and air and clouds and trees
and that the world was the wall.

The End of the Story

Anne, sister Anne, is anyone coming?

The swallows are circling above the woodland
the shadows stir beneath the trees

Anne, sister Anne, what more can you see?

An empty road, brown with dust
a fox that peers from the underbrush

Anne, sister Anne, how far does your gaze reach?

To the meeting-place of forest and sky

But Death is climbing up within—
in all the huge world is there no help?

I see a boy in the stable-yard
he has turned, he's blowing me a kiss

Anne, sister Anne, look again look again!

Two needletips of coppery light
far down the road, are nearing fast
like eyes of a great panther running:
Death's other semblance is in sight

Five

Orpheus to Eurydice

for Laurence Lieberman

1

As you know, I have not lost you.

It would be presumptuous
in the violet evening
to imagine a freedom
apart from the terrors you have designated,

apart from the body's decay,
the cancer hiving within
and the sullen taste of puke
with which the story ends.

2

Less trade now in this city
which I've loved ever since my childhood's
wintry nights—

but an immense bustle of
decay, as peddlers, jugglers
throng the avenues

and I seek to follow the one
of all these millions
who will hand me your gift—

as it were a flower.

3

Many years have passed since Europe,
dying then as always,
sent me the message shielded
by your green-grey eyes.

I drove you out the back roads—do you remember?
and put my arm across your shoulders
tensed slightly under
the white angora.

4

Men are killing men,
they're killing women and children:
whites and yellows are good at it,
blacks and browns catching up fast.
Do you like the touch of blood in your tapestry?

Yes, adored, you do—
and all the more, I expect,
since you can read in their swine-snouts
how ready they are to grovel.

5

Three times I came into you:

in the garden one night of mid-August
when a wind was stirring the shrubs—
on the river's bank while crows were cawing
down a long September afternoon—
and again after the first frost
when the fields had lost their color.

Then you died and rotted.

6

When I went looking for you
the lands were grey and locked:
the straight had been made crooked,
the messages put into code.

It seemed to me, though, that one old crow I saw
in his uneven passage
from bare tree to bald ground
could riddle me out the answer.

7

And the city was a screen of images
that closed you off
in their virtual past:

the childhood park of games
where we played in my made-up country
falling and scraping our knees—
the soiled room where I encountered women
tangy in the sweat of summer
(you were there, in all those women)
and the first songs came.

8

The smoke of the city at night
rising from obscure chimneys
smirches the moon.

A month after you died
I saw a bat skimming
from the cornice of a public building
and followed his lurching flight above the warehouses . . .

He had no message from you.

9

How to make the descent, then,
to your silent mirror?
The old paths are blocked by
history's debris
and we find we dislike the new ones,

their way ever downward
empty of mythologies
with at the end a few bland ghosts
starved to wisps of gesture!

10

And the mystic inner sea
is itself problematic.
I shall find a raft for the crossing, no doubt,
and abandon it on the far side

and making my way through the grey lands
in birdless quiet
attain at the last but a city full
of the shadows of jugglers and peddlers.

11

To find you, to lead you back by the hand,
adored one terrible with claws!
I lust for your haunches
as the old ones lusted for the Sphinx

and am not reconciled
that you be stuffless now
serene in your shadow-pasture
in the last reflex of the mirror—

not reconciled, nor shall be,

12

even though the harsh deaths,
the murders, are continuous
and I do not wish to see the blood
mirrored in your eyes—

even though I well know
you love what is and will be
and may not deflect by an eyelash
the hand that strikes to kill.

13

But see, now,
your eyes are passageways,
your breasts the memories of fullness,
and those strong legs that clasped me thrice
have walked you into the shadows

from which I say I shall reclaim you
lucidly as though
you bore a second history of my ancient self.

14

What remains—my song?
To be bandied among the jugglers
and parceled out by the peddlers, to be sure.

It is something given
as all else is given here—
once in the tangled steaming heap
and once in the mirror.

15

I greet each day as it comes.
May the sun rise and set
with my blessing always
of man and song.
How endless it all is,
how without compunction!

Already I have turned and looked—
and you, already, have been lost again.

Six

"Writing is simplicity..."

Writing is simplicity,
my hand here today
my thought a mirror turning.

Birds in huge families
weave in Geneva trees
fabrics of light sound

as though in choir descended
from the old Areopagite's
sky-blue secret pages

into a tentative now, where
the mirror of things in themselves
is calm in its awaiting...

Let fall the metaphor.
The texture of the day
and fresh wind from the lake

are simple in their presence:
sounds are only sounds
this morning in Geneva,

the birds are hidden in the trees
and hand is quietly itself,
a secret part of me,

as thought moves on
external to my desire,
glad in its cool release.

Thought

for Paula

Any thought at all
      is a good thought today,
the air so fine and chill,
      the sun out, as if meaning to stay—
but for me the thought of you, my dear,
      is the best of all, always—
and I think of you in your plaid skirt
      with top very décolleté—
and the day has its meaning
      and the meaning's here to stay.

The Path

Not that the
caterpillar
yellow with black spines
humping through long grass, knew it
there in the ragged field

nor the aged
barn where
the parson kept his cows,
nor I who walked the borders
twenty minutes slowly

nor any single
mind nor
aptitude of being—
no—the day dissembled
golden in its transience

as the fragile
half-seen
pathway closed again:
not knowing itself there,
there only to be known.

At Midnight

At midnight
at the edge of the point
with the dark waters snuffling about me,
waiting
I raised my head to the stars—
but no word came back
across the years
of strange lives reaching out to mine
at midnight.

At midnight
in the glib wind's stirring
a sudden dread came on me
of space
and the nothing behind my eyes:
I remembered the dead
in their hidden house
but there wasn't a one who could show his face
at midnight.

At midnight
as I walked the rocks
I foresaw great nature's destruction
by slime—
the slime of which I'm made—
and felt my rage
converge within
until this self was one bright point of pain
at midnight.

At midnight
as the tide was turning
I let it all fall into your hand,
Lady,
who are Lord beyond the stars
and who bide your time
to the end of my kind—
you who alone kept watch with me
at midnight.

The Turn

The door of the shed,
   part-way o-
pen, gave out into half-light.

At one side a brown
   paper bag,
half-full of nails, sat crumpled.

The sun had set just
   a minute
or so before, the light was

going fast, the wind
   sifting up
from the shore edged past my head,

leaving at my skin
   its touch of
northern September. Birds on

the move (a few were
   chirping still
outside) would die—so I thought—

thousands, millions in
   emptiness
of passage. How would they not—

those small, precise minds
   fixed on the
one end, not remembering

nests that were cold now?
  And I too
would turn (as red clouds dimmed to

night's all-color) in
  this new can-
niness, sensing how (the mo-

ment of fullness once
  attained) no-
thing remains but withdrawal.

Amitabha

for Paula

An old grey board on the beach at Blue Hill
pink for five minutes in
the Autumn dawn.

After Shen Chou

White clouds, red leaves flying—
I paddle home across the lake.
Alighting on my bow, a crane perches,
measures me with his golden eye.

After Wen Cheng-ming

At sunset the hills turn purple,
the trees drip still from the afternoon rains.

One can sit alone in the long silence,
sit quietly and sing.

Best of all is having nothing to do:
let the world disperse itself!

A narrow path leads up and around—
nearby, we know, is the home of an immortal.

After Su Shih

A whisper echoes
            from the cloud
above a mountain that is not there . . .

Eternity, I

One may define "eternity" in various ways—
as contemplation, say, passion or joy—
but preferably not as a blank stretch that runs on and on.
Quality sums it, not extent.

Call it intensification of the actual
to a point at which, cut free from the known web,
it plunges to its depths within yourself:

or, if you prefer, a process (which seems continuous)
whereby a second world in its reflections
makes real the images of what is now:

or give it, even, the name of nothingness,
the final staring void on which all other
voids may be visaged as transparent masks:

it touched me at all events this afternoon,
an ordinary afternoon in New York City,
in the eye of the blonde child wearing a dark red tam
who looked at me laughing as I returned her ball—

in the meeting, a few blocks further north on Madison,
with a man who had cried in my room twenty years before—
in the sugary smell from the corner bakery store—

in the dream I adventured, asleep here in my chair,
of eating fruit in a jungle patio:
oranges, strawberries from glass bowls decked with mint—

and yet once more, at the clouded time of dusk
when mind, adrift, moved through its nearer voids
and first the diffident poem showed itself.

The Busses

for Paula

From our high window
rainy winter mornings
we see the yellow school-busses
gliding down Park—
darkish, moistly glowing in the rain.

They stop at entries
where children climb aboard
bringing their new-found selves into
that transient space
crowded with a momentary life.

We watch, turn away—
and when in changing light
we look again, we see a stream
dark in China
down which sleek goldfish dart and gleam.

The Message

"This is your life—
it is *not* a dress-rehearsal"
a T-shirt announced.
I have been pondering the message.

One must shoot the works and not hold back—
I'll go along with that—
with giving life what's yours to give.
But having granted this much,

remember your life is after all
not very much yours:
other entities have charge
of primal bodily functions,

of impulses, emotions—
maybe of the way the mind works.
Sometimes you feel you're taking command of it all,
but the feeling doesn't last—

a little pain takes care of that—
and sooner or later you get this other message:
you're going along with it all, you're part of the package,
but it's not *yours*.

You might think of yourself as a coordinator,
or perhaps—more accurately—a "mere observer."
Observer of what?
Of a play—or a dress-rehearsal.

Breath

At the peak of noon the world pauses
(for a moment only) as if
something huge were holding its breath.

A moment only. And a prayer
(as it would be named, were we not afraid of it)
goes up up into that sky

where an old man used to sit on his throne
keeping his eye on things
(but he's sly, he has changed his look) . . .

And the self is caught in silence there,
suspended in its reach
to otherness, and held—

till the moment's life-in-death
passes, and the whole round sum
(mirror of what could not be thought)

breaks into multiplicity:
the randomness of fragments
from which we build the day.

The Mermaid

for Paula

A mermaid there, floating
this cool spring day, above
soiled, square apartment blocks
I look southward upon...

Absurd. No chance of
such sweet happenings!
Something, though, with breasts and
flowing hair is sunning herself

right now in this bright New York air
as though just having surfaced
from everyone's unconscious...
Do you suppose she has something

to tell us, my dear,
of how she will protect those
who visit her beneath the tides,
but can't be coaxed to yield her name?

Seven

Century Poem

for A. R. Ammons

I

When the Wheel of the century turned from light to dark
the ghost of Poe rose chattering in Baltimore
and rayed black panic over the drugged lands

the Baptist walked, with lizards in his hands

and a Sphinx upreared her head beside the White House:
>   *Sekhet-Aaru Utchat Re*
>   I am the child of yesterday
>   *Cor sva jo* man sprouts from slime
>   blood wells up through the sluice of time
>   *Impavidum ferient ruinae*

Above the central plains the sky turned silver
with cyclones simmering from a sensitive source
and blood rained down on Topeka with fish and frogs

The President became a vegetarian

and the Sphinx half-smiled, as a bat crawled from her mouth
unlimbered its black sails
and sported in the Washington air with the President's helicopter—
meanwhile, the gentlemen of the Highway Lobby got down on all fours
like little elephants in a chain
and crawled one by one nose first into the brown
Potomac (already heavily polluted)

—Tell on, my song, the *annus mirabilis!*
Eggs and pale blood on the peaks of Oregon
old yellow women back-packing in Death Valley
and a limbo of fog on the starved manufacturing towns
soot of Wilmington, slough of Newark
Jersey chemical dumps and Massachusetts mills

The Specter walked...

                    and walks the quiet hills
of a lost Connecticut, calm summers of the past
undying dreams, unfailing faces, as memory holds fast
in full elation of the Sphinx's glare

I shall not speak my murders to this air . . .

In Vermont a stone-age tribe shambled down from the Green
    Mountains—
bloat-skulled, chalk-faced, mumbling an unformed speech
they massacred the retired professors, ate cows raw in the fields

2
                    The ghost of Poe sang "Muley muley
                    I love Lenore, I love her truly
                    Dauntless I seek my lost Lenore
                    through the dim streets of Baltimore"

                    The doubleghost sang "Mene penny
                    I love her not, I love not any
                    Quenchless I follow, near and far
                    my lost god Monsieur Valdemar"

A chess-player of steel, seven storeys tall in front of the Plaza
(his head was planted with a small rock-garden)
mated Bobby Fischer on a King's Indian and swallowed him alive—
a thousand golden hawks appeared in the blue air of New York
and proceeded to decimate the pigeon population
(to the delight of Miss Farida A. Wiley)
while in the Museum of Natural History
strange movements were reported from the back corridors:
scorpions of glass, vanessids of pure copper
exchanging curt messages at ultra-high frequencies
proconsuls stirring in the furry dark
mouthing dull syllables, summoning back to flesh
the starvelings of old evil Olduvai—
everywhere, manifestations of an intention

74

(*whose* intention is not to be revealed)
in shrieks of skittish school-children tricked out in parrot feathers
in tinglings of the brontosaurus bones
in the solemn stride of statues heaving their borrowed breaths

. . . And from the steps of St. Patrick's Cathedral
the ghost of Cardinal Spellman, naked and obese
displayed its bloated buttocks to the ranks of passing veterans

(An Angel saw it from on high
poised in the sky above the Chrysler Building—
a six-winged smiler with corundum eyes)

3
. . . There's a whisper of yellowy-green on the trees in Central Park
the half-breed lovers wait for dark
the birds sing *ki-ri-ki* and *koo-roo-koo*

Gold chessmen litter the floor of the Stock Exchange

and Poe's ghost scours the streets of Baltimore
in search of his cousins of latter days
in search of the wraith-white blouse of his lost Lenore
(in search of that sinister frog Monsieur Valdemar, what's more)

And the beggars have taken over in California—
with mouths full of orange they bugger the Hollywood starlets
and ride bare-assed on starving desert nags
Disaster! What new star swirls over Palomar
injecting its hyaline rays into the palaver of astronauts:
Col. Glenn, Col. Armstrong, Col. Teilhard de Chardin
Col. Tolstoy, Col. Gandhi, Col. Guillaume Apollinaire
Col. Grossefesse, Col. Baise-mon-cul—what star
sings glitter-tongued the lotus lands of space?

> *On Planet X the dawns move sluggish*
> *up from the steaming chlorine seas*

> The people wave their fibrous arms
> in infraspectral harmonies
>
> On Planet X they take their sex
> unmixed with love's frivolities
> In violet gloom their mighty mergings
> quell all at once the mind's unease

In a New York of the twenties, in a flat near Washington Square
after engaging in perverse forms of intercourse
Justine in her mask hears the quiet song of the planets
> *al lah   ah lah   ah loooooo*
and tastes the desire of the boy who yearns for the Green Star
high, high in the tingling night above One Fifth Avenue

. . . The raggy men are dreaming on park benches
Snow falls on Washington Arch
> flake
> > flakelet
> > > flake

4
Cor sva jo   The winged ones built their palaces of skulls
in California parceled into lots
while Liszt's *Les Preludes* brayed out over the housing projects
and the lord with zircon cuffs at his piano
tinkled a nocturne to the fiberglass flowers

> In Houston, in the Astrodome
> the Werewolves played the Frankensteins
> The Franks touched down a hundred times
> stomping and crushing wolfish bones
>
> The bleeding fiends shrieked black despair
> which stopped the monsters in their tracks
> A hundred heads were wrenched from necks
> sailed through the murk to tie the score

And from across the Rio Grande a living slime
uneasy, putrescent, invaded the plains of Texas—
a porridge of eyes and dismembered parts, a scum of yelping mouths
it devoured the oil-men and ranchers and their expensive sons and
  daughters

The President, attempting to cope with the situation
convoked in Washington an assembly of eminent Poets:
for three days (all expenses paid) they met and mumbled
choice passages from their Collected Shirts and Selected Warts

and Mr. Rockefeller demanded the Baptist's head on a platter
to be reproduced in majestic enlargement at the top of Number One
  World Trade Center
whence, gazing out across the harbor—
this was all in the interests of American Democracy, of course—
it might be expected to exchange intelligence with the Statue of Liberty
(while at the top of Number Two a pallid bust was revealed)

The Congress then, in solemn session, voted itself a raise
the President read Longfellow, regretting the old ways
the Sphinx flew to New Mexico to fast for forty days

(the Poets had no answers
but awarded one another nevertheless the customary medals and prizes)

and the Atlantic rolled its breakers on the Carolina shores
the Atlantic full of jellyfish and molluscs
the Atlantic rolled its breakers on the broken coast of Maine—
the ghost of Poe went floating, dreaming in the rain

5

A friendly rubber at the Whist Club
Valdemar trumps Poe's hopeless ace
The black cat on the bust of Pallas
frets with his tail the marble face

Poe bears his disappointment staunchly
courteously he quits the game
Meanwhile Maria spreads her haunches—
this time a Raven takes the blame

And dancing dancing dancing on the mall in Central Park
three naked girls outfling arms breasts and thighs
black red and blonde their pubic hair
Alice and Cynthia and Lenore—
a few children watch, a mounted policeman, with benevolence—
for the moment the sun is shining, it is warm in the city
as dwarfish sails speckle the glinting ponds

    Yes, I have seen the lost Lenore
    Long-haired she walks nocturnal streets
    holding two afghans on a leash
    She's fair, she hasn't all her wits

And a soi-disant Christ is born in New Mexico, in the desert
spawned of the Sphinx and Valdemar the Raven—
he feeds the ghosts of old prospectors on cactus milk
he picks up lizards in his hands and lets them go again
stakes out no claims, seeks out no souls
cries "Back to hell, man!" to the ghost of Cardinal Spellman
and has never been half in love with easeful death . . .
He drinks pure broth, he draws pure breath
signs a compact of friendship with the people of Acoma Pueblo
watches admiringly the girls swinging topless in the bordertown bars
writes good-humored letters to the Editor of The New York Times
and when Angels drift in on cloudbanks from the north
glides up beside them in his shimmering shirt

6

Be careful, ladies and gentlemen, or you may be hurt—
everything these days is not what it seems
(as you very well know) including the warning signs
so pay no attention to this poem, no attention at all

The wheel moves on regardless, night and day
and if you're on it, you have to go its way—
no one's making you hold on though, so why not try letting go?

. . . It was just off Madison Avenue the message came
one May afternoon, the specter walking beside me
appeased for a moment by delicacies of Spring—
an Angel brought it; small, female, rather French-looking
dressed in high fashion, wearing a tourmaline
she stopped on the sidewalk smiling and handed me a telegram

With respect to your understanding of the universe
this is to inform you that there seem to be many errors
imbedded in your habitual ways of thinking and feeling
In certain areas things are better than you allow
in others they are much worse

For Angels, Sphinxes, Pterodactyls and so forth the outlook is quite favorable
The World of Ideas is expected to survive
and the mineral realm as well, falling back on its old transmutations—
but as for the rest!
                    Try thinking of something else
like why it should be necessary for you to think at all
this very day and moment

                    No answer was expected—
or desired?

Sunlight on pavement   emptiness of forms
above the Chrysler Building the sky still highly attentive
as a thousand cities eloquent in their absence
renewed these trumperies of human touch . . .

No answer was forthcoming—that much is plain—
but the angel was a changeling, and remains

Eight

The End

Come
this evening
while the snow
is silently evil outside
and the coachman's black-hatted ghost
twirls in bright moonlight frosty mustachios
to the dead place behind the barn
where the Ford's buckled corpse is rusting away
and the children abandoned that heap of broken toys
that will never be repaired, no never in any world,

and celebrate with me the feast of the immaculate destruction
of all the appearances and appurtenances of this life
which seemed for many years a substantial reality
so validly textured of persons places songs
it merited devotion—but which fatally
now, steady as our breathing,
sinks into sacred nothingness
where only one's
other self
remains

The Ghost

It was night, and the mist
came in from the harbor
of that out-of-date town
that had changed but little since I was a child.

The house looked on the central square
where a street-lamp glowed in the darkness:
my old friend, A. B.,
had given me the key.

No one about but a stray dog running
who swerved at me, then slunk away
as I climbed those stone steps slowly,
watched by blind windows from each side.

At the top I paused, my huge key
exerting strength at the front-door lock—
it grated, gave; I walked on through
to echoings dulled in dankish space

and stood for a while in the dim front hall
breathing old dust, letting my eyes
calm themselves to that inner dark.
Then I pulled the big door shut.

I wished to let the silence deepen
around me, to become part of it—
as though it might prove friendlier
the more restrained I showed myself.

The lamplight leaked through soiled panes.
Narrowly, I saw a black
doorway gaping to my right
and up ahead steep stairs ascending.

I have you now, I thought. I shall
not let you pass unless you bless me.
Followed my torch through the sideward rooms—
found nothing. Started up the stairs.

Half-way up my light went out
and I whiffed a foulness drifting down.
I gagged. Something snuffled up there
not far above me. I felt despair,

as though from a sickness long-forgotten
that would kill me yet—then at my ears
a harsh dark whisper: "Be on your way.
Leave me, fool, you may not stay."

I took two more steps all the same
through fog clotting at my face and hair:
the old ghost smelled of earthenware,
I felt his hatred gnawing me.

"Bless me, old rotting sire," I said,
"bless me, and I will let you be."
But he came on faceless with a groan
and as I clutched the icy rail

in a chill rush he brushed me by
and plunging through the hollowed house,
fled moaning out into his night . . .

My light came on. I was alone.

Eternity, II

I have found it.
          What?
Eternity.
It is the city
mingled with sun.

Speak not of flight,
unquiet guardian,
when the still shadow
cancels all bets

and statues stride
these virid parks
beneath the hawks'
gold-glinting wings:

for self assumes
annihilation
of the great orb's
assertive fire,

and sea has gone!
The earth goes, too.
Courage remains
and a last knowledge

of breathings, dark
behind night's glass—
twinges, threats
of star-borne pain.

I have found it.
          What?
Eternity.
It is the city
turned to night.

"Lucky black man in my dream..."

for Rosemary Felton

Lucky black man in my dream
drove me up the vast turnpike
in his galactic taxicab:
all through the night we were headed home.

A rabbit's foot hung from the mirror,
an emerald glittered at his ear,
he hummed an easy-going tune—
"Sail on, Dupree, sail on sail on..."

Our voyaging was south to north.
We crossed a gash where Jersey was
and threaded a tiny river town
whose streets were crooked and thick with mist.

Stopped at a bar for a glass of beer.
The place was jammed, they were singing songs,
my daughter was there, quick-stepping with friends—
she danced up and took the black man's hand.

He gave me a wink, and said, "Come along,
the last lap's ahead, not a moment to lose,
we'll make it together before morning comes.
You hadn't a friend, but now you're strong."

Then under the river and huge with speed
we stabbed through the dark like a striking snake
and surfaced in Manhattan easy and free
before a man or a house was awake!

Lucky black man in my dream
drove me through the night-hushed streets
in his dawning taxicab
as the lights changed red to green...

All the lights changed red to green—
we never stopped, we never paused,
but crossed the city we had won
returning to the dream of home.

President Poem

A President appeared to me in dreams
solemn-seeming as an undertaker
but unpredictable.

I came across him first ten years ago
sitting in the upholstered cave
of an old black Packard town-car parked at random
late at night in the porte-cochere at Borderland
before the old house was torn down.
He was on the alert, reading a stack of mail
while the black-capped driver waited onyx-eyed
up front. Slow winds crept through the pines
to where I watched invisibly observant,
and while I watched, two owls flew overhead.
He read his letters in the dark
calmly with a settled look,
one at a time. He had all the time in the world
it seemed—and nothing now or ever would escape him.

Next at an evening gathering—
champagne, décolletage, and all the rest—
we met in someone's mansion in Vienna
(or maybe Paris: Faubourg St. Honoré).
The sleek dark sideboards glowed
with carved decanters glinting candlelight
as half-seen shapes sidled past murmuring
and a tall black man white-tied at the piano
dismembered Liszt in elegant cascades...
Then all at once the President stood up
(for a moment resembling Holbein's Thomas More)
and leaving his little group of six or seven,
laughingly led me out onto the terrace
where suddenly the sun blazed out full strength.

(Two visions—or one real thing twice seen?
I never asked what the President could mean
but trusted in the climates I encountered
to lend my thoughts their subtle definition.)

I saw him last early in a year of change.
I sat in a huge stadium
packed with the living and the dead
and watched two shadowy armies play at football.
The stakes were high: would dead and living live
for ever in such precincts as I dreamed
or fall for ever through oubliettes of night?
The score was tied . . . And then he came on field
in stiff dark business suit and low black shoes,
stepped back, took a short run, and kicked the goal
after his dim precursors all had failed.

The Summit

for Paula

If you've just once been happy,
you have the right to assume
you're out of the reach of destruction.

I read that somewhere once and
didn't believe it at all
for happiness as I knew it was

only a point, quickly passed,
on the common road that leads
(as far as one can survey it) to

destruction and nowhere else.
What reasoning was this, which
would deny our time as we've lived it

and make us hostages to
assumptions no one has proved?
What can it possibly mean, to say

that those who once were happy
can "bear to die"? I wonder.
Why wouldn't it be all the harder

since they're asked to give up more?
It's those who are sick, wretched,
sunk in pain, who are ready to quit—

like my poor friend Costello,
at Hood back in '44,
who screamed so from his hospital bed

he burst a vein in his throat.
Destruction was fine by him . . .
But I've got the argument twisted—

I see it now all at once—
for plain willingness to die
isn't the point. The point is rather

whether, in someone's life, it
may come to pass that the self
reach a place of high vantage from which,

as from a mountain meadow,
future and past recede, and
the road itself lose its meaning. If

so, when the life is resumed,
something is left behind there
(wedded to the high place for ever)

which knows itself as lasting
beyond the self that moves on:
a thing at home in its happiness

as an oak tree is at home
in its own rich-textured shade,
or as an old fish deep in ocean

is at home, flexing his way
effortlessly, without thought . . .
And this thing it is which remains and

remembers itself and time
moving to their destruction
in the self which they seek to rejoin.

Poetry from Illinois

History Is Your Own Heartbeat
Michael S. Harper (1971)

The Foreclosure
Richard Emil Braun (1972)

The Scrawny Sonnets and Other
Narratives
Robert Bagg (1973)

The Creation Frame
Phyllis Thompson (1973)

To All Appearances: Poems New and
Selected
Josephine Miles (1974)

Nightmare Begins Responsibility
Michael S. Harper (1975)

The Black Hawk Songs
Michael Borich (1975)

The Wichita Poems
Michael Van Walleghen (1975)

Cumberland Station
Dave Smith (1977)

Tracking
Virginia R. Terris (1977)

Poems of the Two Worlds
Frederick Morgan (1977)

Images of Kin: New and Selected
Poems
Michael S. Harper (1977)

On Earth As It Is
Dan Masterson (1978)

Riversongs
Michael Anania (1978)

Goshawk, Antelope
Dave Smith (1979)

Coming to Terms
Josephine Miles (1979)

Local Men
James Whitehead (1979)

Death Mother and Other Poems
Frederick Morgan (1979)